Reflections

Isanne Zoller

A Book of Poems by
Isanne Zoller

Reflections

Library of Congress
Cataloging in Publication Data

ISBN 0-7951-0449-9

Manufactured in The United States of America by
Watermark Press
6 Gwynns Mill Court
Owings Mills, MD 21117
410-654-0400

*This book is lovingly dedicated
to my beautiful granddaughters
Belinda and Teresa Zoller*

Introduction

While "Reflections" is Isanne Zoller's first book, she has had poems written in many anthologies. As for these poems, she has received many awards, trophies and plaques for her endeavors.

After WWII, her parents had to flee from Indonesia to Israel. There, she was born in a little town named Hadera. After a period of nearly three years, the family was finally admitted to America.

At that point the family settled in Chicago, IL, and through her father, George Rosenberg, (a concert pianist and college music professor,) she began a childhood career in dancing on live television shows, on stage and concerts. However, after many health problems and finally diagnosed with Multiple Sclerosis, she could no longer perform.

In 1970 she married her husband Joseph and were later blessed with a son (Joe Jr.) who is now married and with his lovely wife Stacey have two daughters, Belinda and Teresa.

Still having the desire to be part of the Arts, she found her outlet in writing and poetry has given her the feeling of being an artist once again.

According to Isanne, "Being able to express one's thoughts in different ways can be very rewarding. It allows people to read their own feelings and share the magic of words with others."

A to Z Index

A Little Bit Of Heaven

Soothing caresses from your arms of brown,
Gently touched and probed by your finger tips of green,
Holding me close to your warm, ample bosom,
Clutching me tightly 'til I become serene.

Dusting me softly with the rays of the sun,
Rocking to and fro in your cradle of love,
I'm enveloped in a blanket made of clouds,
Moonbeams shining down with stars twinkling above.

Birds fly overhead inviting me, "Come play!"
Squirrels and chipmunks scurry all about me,
Flowers opening their scented petals,
Their aromas spread by the wind and the bee.

Suckled at the breast of dear Mother Nature,
My back kept straight by the support of the trees,
Curiosity always answered in full,
By looking up to the skies, out to the sea.

Running and jumping with animals by day,
Then cuddled in a bed so rich, plush and right,
I am again enclosed in a wonderful manner,
Wrapped in the cloak of love by day and by night.

A New Home For Everyone

I'm sitting wrapped in the warmth of the coolness,
There's an aura that makes everyone feel good,
The enjoyment of the place itself is amazing,
The only ones that can't enjoy it must be made of wood.

There you can have the company of family,
No, you are not genetically united,
People can become close with total strangers
And secrets can be comfortably confided.

The world doesn't offer a great deal of security,
Even close friends aren't always safe with each other,
Sometimes it is easier to talk to unknown folds,
Most of the time it's also better than a brother.

Ah, the pure art of basking in love can be done,
There is indeed a shortage of people who show they care,
It's something that no country offers their own,
It doesn't even make it possible for them to share.

A Piece Of The Past

Memories can be beautiful and so kind,
Memories can be as cozy as an old shirt,
They can be funny and start one giggling,
But memories can also be cruel, and hurt.

A person must decide which they would like to keep,
One must choose the right path to prevent sadness,
Hug closely the memories of happiness and fun,
For only a fool would prefer the madness.

Have a mind full of laughter and joy to bring smiles,
Have a soul grinning in the warmth of contentment,
Have a heart swelling with love, pride and peace eternal,
Put aside all the pain, fears and resentment.

Eyes that glisten with tears of the enchanted,
Features that can be soft as that of a sprite,
Hold fast to that babe who loaned you his dreams
Never say good-by to that, only good night.

A Poem For Peace

I know that we have all been given the gift of love,
It was given to us from the God above,
Yet, as humans we fight over the dumbest things,
Like who has more money or diamond rings.

I don't know when or why this insanity started,
Unfortunately, people have become quite hard hearted,
They have stolen but worse, they have killed one of yours,
For silly things like, ground, homes and joys of wars.

There are more children being born each day,
But, most have no one to show them the way,
While so many people feel their religion is right,
They think nothing of insulting those
with whom they fight.

God did not mean to have so many sects say
they are the special ones,
Collecting funds can't be the way,
for too many have none,
Why, in a world so beautiful
must man destroy the very best?
I sincerely hope, God, that You can find time to rest.

A Sad Stage Of Life

Why is he treating her like that?
What did she ever do to him
Except take care of his every need
And cater to his every whim.

She gave and gave 'til there was no more,
Her strength, her soul and all her love,
He can't see that what she wanted
Was only to be like a hand in glove.

What she asked him to do was difficult,
But she thought he could be strong and able to do it.
He wouldn't even try to change things,
Instead of even a lame attempt, he said he couldn't do it.

The strangest part is it was for him
that she wanted it done,
So they could be together for a long time,
But he stormed out with an attitude,
To which there was no rhythm, no rhyme.

So now they are both sad and each is alone,
And each is in a different place,
Both heading in opposite directions,
Walking an unsure, slow, tenuous pace.

Isanne Zoller

Alone Again, Forever

As I wander through years of memories,
I can't help but feel sad,
While some still cause me pain,
Truly, not all of it was bad.

If one can grieve for times never to be again,
Then it is my heart that will cry,
For I can't repeat the past and
All of the times, with me, will die.

I prayed that you would recall our happy times,
Selective memory is no longer a catch phrase,
It now describes the way your mind works,
How can you forget so many days?

By my age, you'd think I would be used to it,
But sometimes it seems as though we've just met,
But, being who I am, I shall always mourn,
All those times you were able to forget.

At Last!

How did I ever let that get control?
I don't recall feeling any loss,
But, there it was, missing one day,
And I was no longer the boss.
It doesn't sadden me but it is confusing,
For that part doesn't even know it's not there,
That goes on with life not realizing
Because that part doesn't really care.

For me, it's a new side of liberty,
One I was so afraid to long for,
Now, as my own creator,
I want to be free all the more.
I love now knowing I can do it,
It is infiltrating my entire existence;
I started feeling a bit off balance,
But, now I offer no resistance.

Do I really want the ability?
To direct one's self can be scary,
I can, hopefully, do many things to help,
My degrees of assistance will vary.
I have truly found me,
The old me that I cared about,
Not someone who is mean or bitter,
Just someone I thought I could live without.

But, here I am and here I will remain,
Why should I change when this is where I will stay?
I do hope you love me when I'm like this,
Because this is how I shall be forever and a day.

Autumn's End

Leaves slowly floating by on their way down,
Making sure they have time to wave farewell,
Then they fall to the ground as if they knew
Exactly where to land to create their tapestry.

Each tree's leaves are oh, so many shades,
That blend and complement one another,
They take a single color and its tint,
Then show the multihues of nature's palette.

A few leaves only descend to others,
Small ones shining like jewels on a green tray,
But soon the bigger leaves will also turn
And the gems will finally fall to the earth.

Every leaf knows it has served its purpose,
They are not scared or sad about their fate,
The sharing of their beauty is their way
Of acknowledging that **God** knows what is best.

Beware Of...

Question me never about things I cannot tell,
Ignorance is a cloak you wear so very well,
These stories should be at the bottom of a well,
Or, at least, locked up in a darkened cell.

For when I heard these tales, 'twas on my knees I fell,
And it was in the background I could hear the bell,
Both of my legs felt as if they were gel,
So quivered beneath me in a manner pell-mell.

Then, a stranger asked me if my soul I would sell,
I tripped on my coat's hem and rolled down to the dell,
Where I heard the sound of a rather nearby bell,
Hoping someone was close, I began to yell.

The response was silence, for no one heard me yell,
Overwhelmed by despair, the tears from my eyes, fell,
I heard chimes and, again, was asked my soul to sell,
I said yes, and the ringing became, once more, the knell.

Bittersweet

It's a reminder of days gone by,
It's an example of how dreams die,
A dose of reality of hopes gone astray,
A nagging voice of judgment following a happy day.

Every day that goes by should bring someone happiness,
Yet, every encounter serves to be nothing but a test,
The human spirit endures so much before it dies,
But it lingers on, waiting for answers to the whys.

Must the soul continually pray for a reprieve?
Who will lose all that is given if there's a plot to deceive?
Alas, the gentle heart will be the one sacrificed,
Who but the trusting fool would believe them,
but they lied.

Indeed, it turned out all that sparkled was not gold,
But the innocent went along with what it was told,
Standing erect, begging to please with eyes full of tears,
Pretending to be brave and strong
but consumed with fears.

Devastated, forlorn and empty was the broken heart,
It should, but couldn't, run away from the cold steel dart,
Falling on its knees, gasping for air, the naïve cried,
All the while it wanted nothing more
than to be one who died.

Can We?

Can we ever truly forgive each other?
Problems in a family are sometimes nothing but a fuss,
What about when we hear and know things
about murders,
How can we ever forgive it if it's aimed at us?

How can one man be in charge of all of our lives?
What makes him think he is the one to rule?
Aren't God, Allah, Jehovah not the same being?
Is man any different than a tool?

Are we not all blessed with life by a supreme being?
How can anyone say that we aren't the same?
What are we, all of us, looking for?
Is this just a ploy or a joke, or someone's sick game?

The pattern of man is hard to follow even for the wise,
There are ups when there should be downs,
Who ever the puppet controller is
He's making us all look like clowns.

The wish or prayer to let us realize we are all one,
Is there any magic that can help us to change the world?
Or shall we end up leaving a legacy, an imprint,
Or will it be a flag just hanging there unfurled?

7/14/2001

Childhood – Terminated

I read an article about a child, who will never grow old,
He was tortured and beaten by his parent
who loved him,
He will never be able to play with other children,
He will never play football nor will he ever swim.

He will never learn to ride a bike or a horse,
He won't break any records or break any glasses,
He won't pretend he is a policeman or sheriff,
Nor will he grow up to go to any college classes.

We will never see his smile when he loses his teeth,
We will never know if he was going to be tall,
We won't have a chance to see him score
the winning goal,
We won't be able to see him pick himself up after a fall.

We will never read anything written by this child,
We will never see a painting signed by this boy,
We will never have to teach him about history,
And we will never have to buy him a toy.

He won't have to decide if he wants to get married,
He will never laugh again nor will he have to cry,
He will never have to worry about his future, will he?
And we will never have to say good-bye.

Depression

Were I but a plaster statue grotesquely displayed,
'twould be far easier to accept neglect.
My awareness seeks to destroy
Albeit the very core of my existence.
Could someone not save the damsel in distress?
She crieth out in pain, "Protect me from me."

They listen, not understanding,
Nor accepting, they have no time.
She's dying, feels no one sorrow?
Do they not see the demise of their own?
Lonely business, this loving.

Pouring out my soul is for naught,
I speak of foreign things.
Emotions deemed deniable, forbidden,
But not for me, let them flow freely,
Fear not ye must reply in full measure,
I ask for but a pittance.

Reward my stupidity with kindness,
Answer my urgency
But with an acknowledgement,
Say not "Tis too much!"
I fade quickly,
I am not.

Destroyed

My thoughts are pounding like jackhammers in my head,
I scream in silence and from every orifice I bleed,
It is the respect I should receive that I am denied,
Told, that I must talk to walls despite what I need.

I shouldn't be so hurt when you yell these words,
For I know that the walls won't take pleasure in my pain,
The walls of this house are not the prison of my heart,
The prison is you, all these years of love feigned.

My heart is crying from thoughts of how it should've been,
Memories start as happy times
but then the darkness comes,
Coming to the end of that day becomes overwhelming,
Then the good feelings are pushed to the when and from.

You have played me for a fool all too many years,
Yet it still goes on and now
you have gained an accomplice.
Now all the hurt is not divided, it is multiplied,
And these dreadful memories I wish I had missed.

I am not a child and loathe being treated as one,
The slaps across my mind are more painful
than you could know,
There is a big empty spot in my life where you should be,
But I can't let you in until I know if you're friend or foe.

Dreams

Covet me, dear soul of my dreams,
Tell me all of your plans and schemes,
Will you hold me close to your heart?
And, promise me we'll never part?

Will we travel around the world?
Into the stars, will we be hurled?
As clouds, shall we orbit the earth?
To follow the line at its girth?

Can we fly upward to the moon?
But, may we come back very soon?
In a garden, can we then rest?
And as children, will we be dressed?

Will we wear crowns on our heads?
Can we do all the things that you said?
Would you caress me with your touch?
For I love you so very much.

Isanne Zoller

Dressing For The Season

To whom it may concern, the trees are going bald!
Yes, I know that spring will be coming soon,
But, those trees are getting older now and
Through their bare branches, I saw the moon.

I know that this is something I shouldn't worry about,
But it breaks my heart when things like this occur,
Those beautiful colors won't be seen 'til next year,
Right now, all that I'm seeing, I see through a blur!

I can't help crying, letting tears run down my cheeks,
But, perhaps if I were taller or perhaps if trees could sit,
I could gather the foliage and make a leaf-piece,
I would sort out the leaves and make sure each wig fit.

Well if **God** meant it to be so, who am I to complain?
I suppose the trees and I could discuss the recent past,
We could reminisce about their fall beauty and sigh,
And then say how sad that it couldn't forever more last.

Oh! Then we could talk about what colors
next year they'd wear,
In the excitement, even talk about which shades of green
They would wear in the spring and all summer long,
How in the fall, they'd wear the most breath-taking colors
we've ever seen.

You see, that's exactly what I've been talking about,
If you had a phone, I certainly would have called,
For if you read this, To Whom It May Concern,
*Then you'd know, **Again** the trees are going bald!*

Enough Is Enough

When is it my turn to be the other adult?
It seems that only when things are going badly,
Only when sacrifices must be made, I'm asked,
All those time of hard work I'd exchange most gladly.

When it comes to bad times, you find me easily,
I'm twice adult age but you treat me like a child,
You discuss major situations with another,
When I ned to know what's happened,
you say, "It's filed."

When a decision turns out to be the wrong one,
When you tell me about it, it's always too late,
Then you tell me all that I can't get and can't do,
I have to give up things and then I'm told to wait.

I'm always told about things when it's a done deal,
I'm asked quite meanly how would I have handled it,
I'm told how you don't like this house and/or my cats,
And how if it were not for me, your work you would quit.

In case I wasn't hurt enough by all these things,
The other one announces they had a rotten childhood.
I've sacrificed, given up and given away,
To make your and the other's lives as nice as I could.

I've given you and the other everything I could,
And if any of you needed me to give my blood, I would.

Eternally At Peace

I've been here before I came into that world,
There's such comfort in knowing I'll be with them again,
They brought me so very much happiness in our years,
There was a great deal of laughter but, also some tears.

This unique relationship had no strings attached,
We could be ourselves with no fear of judgment,
There was no competition to darken our way,
No hurtful things did any of us say.

It was a life that had all of us being honest,
None ever felt they were excluded from anything,
Some may have thought this can't be what we truly had,
There had to be, at least, one of us who was bad.

How could it be anything other than perfection?
Wasn't this place the much-envied valley of love?
When we were held closely to that warm, tender heart,
Life became a way of never being apart.

So, to complain was foolish for all we had,
We never went without love and everyone cared,
We were in a place where everyone's dream came true,
For we were in the heaven created by You.

Everyone's Child

I won't tell you how to be a good parent,
But, I will teach you how to be a good child.
This has nothing to do with being mean or nice,
Or even about letting little ones run wild.

This is not about the loss of admiration,
Nor is it about the way you talk to me,
It is about the way you give away words and looks,
That, I hope, that you have no reason to be.

There is something that is very amiss,
You don't want and can't be eye to eye,
Every word is sharp and in a bitter tone,
And all would be fine if I wouldn't be I.

You don't have to perform whenever you see me,
And being civil doesn't hurt very much,
I promise no to embrace you,
But don't be disgusted or cringe at my touch.

Look at your children and age them twenty years,
Are you raising them with genuine love and concern?
And is there anybody else who could tell you how?
Now that is the lesson you should learn.

Do you truly feel the way you are doing it is right?
Or, is this the way that it is meant to be done.
Have you any doubts in your performance,
Or are they your planets and you, their sun?

Don't judge me or criticize me,
My road was a much harder and longer way,
My mistakes have given you an advantage,
You have it easier every single day.

There's plenty of room and time for judging,
Don't lose respect before you know all practicality.
Be proud of your parenting skill,
Just remember you must have a lot of room for reality.

Isanne Zoller

Forever My Child

Cry my child so that I may find you,
I will know you by your eyes of blue,
My precious baby, where have you gone?
The search for you is never done.

The first time I cradled you I knew
A love that can only be true,
And though you have grown to be a man,
I will give you all the love I can.

While at times your heart closes to me,
It hurts that this you want me to see,
For being a parent is quite hard,
And it often leaves your soul marred.

But unlike physical scars that stay,
Wounds of the heart often go away.
The bandage of a hug and a kiss
Brings that love that you'll never want to miss.

Parent and child must think in advance,
Each word and look is taking a chance.
If what we say is meant to cause pain,
Then, perhaps it is love that we feign.

Going Home As A Guest

She's returning home to say her final good bye,
It's been overdue for all these many years,
She never thought or planned to stay away this long,
Now she must face her anxiety and fears.

Possibly she will run into ghosts of back then,
The relics of good and bad memories of the past,
She left as a child but now is a woman,
She's hoping only good feelings will last.

Perhaps all hurt of then will be pushed to the back,
Could be as an adult she'll feel in control,
She can choose what she can or cannot handle,
For her past has already taken its toll.

She has paid for all things, many not her doing,
Still they all haunt her mind and her soul.
She's overcome so many devils and demons,
All she wants is to rid herself of these foes.

Isanne Zoller

She wears a mask that she is brave and strong,
While inside she only shivers and shakes,
Those things she won't let the world see,
She must do this no matter what it takes.

She steels her spine and clenches her fist,
She will battle these dragons so that she can be free,
She'll fight as a daughter to mother, child to adult,
So off she goes as ready as she'll ever be.

Growing Old

Imprisoned by walls that once were a home,
The verdict came the morning past,
Not believing the words that were said then,
They were tumbling, jumbling so fast.

At one time, getting away was so easy,
Or was it just the way it seemed?
Devastation can come in many ways,
The end of things once dreamed.

Dreams are laughed at when you become old,
Friends chortle at all your plans,
Loved ones say stick with what you can do best,
Like laundry and dishes and pans.

What happened to the knight who would save you?
And where is his beautiful steed?
When was his armor traded for a t-shirt
And the rose for an ugly weed?

Protect future generations and dreams,
Let them not repeat this nightmare,
Let us dispel the myth of our knight
And be as honest as we dare.

Hope, No More

Can't believe it's back to the old way,
Still hurtful, still mean,
Fighting to survive but still green,
It has its price to pay.

Can't afford it so now must stop,
Just can't keep up the pace,
Takes too much work and no breathing space,
Can't run, nor jump, nor hop.

Why keep on trying when all is lost?
Stuff loses its charm fast,
Now the present becomes the past,
Couldn't get it at any cost.

Some were too many to have to deal,
Nothing makes sense anymore,
Everything starts to hurt, feel sore,
Not enough strength and everything's too real.

As all begins to accumulate,
No way is the way out,
Searing pain creates more doubt,
Please say this is not an act of fate.

How Could You!

How can you be so indifferent to those who care,
Is there no room in your heart for anyone?
Did God make a mistake when you were born or
Are you just a mean someone?

There doesn't seem to be any room for others,
Not even for those you say you love.
Instead of bemoaning your predicament,
Why don't you seek help from the man above?

You seem to think that the world owes you,
Unfortunately for you, it does not.
You only get back what you give
And you care only for what you've got.

There is little pleasure in your life,
That, even a blind man can see,
For all your phony generosity,
You only care for one, the one that you call "me."

The only ones that will be there for you
Are people who will be there out of pity,
For they will know your true character,
And, that picture will not be pretty.

Isanne Zoller

I Am A Dancer

Forgive my way of walking,
I know that I have shuffled,
I want to scream but
My voice, they have muffled.

I don't know how I look,
For I haven't got a mirror,
I know it's not right,
Someone made a big error.

I'm delicate and graceful,
Quite the lady and refined,
I'm petite and demure,
As if **you,** *I must remind.*

My partner is handsome,
My tutu light blue,
Now if only I could remember,
What I am to do.

I start with a plié,
And then I will run,
And then, I will leap,
Oh! Golly, what fun!!

I can't find my partner,
I did hear a splat,
Okay, so I'm not so svelte,
Maybe, I'm a little fat.

If you were watching and truly believed,
That by my partner I would be caught,
Then have a seat and look at the map,
I got 300 acres of swamp that need to be bought!!!

It's Time

Why blame me for everything that has gone wrong?
Haven't you noticed I don't sing that song,
Anymore.

Your treat me as if I were no more than a child,
The one that upon whom your misery you've piled,
Never more.

If you do treat me as a wee one, then do,
But don't change my position from one place to two,
No more.

I've wondered if you would be able to see that I've aged,
If you look very closely you will see that I've changed,
Each day, more.

Please throw away that broken clock and
join me in the today,
If you cannot find it, let me take your hand
and lead the way,
For evermore.

Jewels Of The Season

The gems of winter will be with us soon,
Crystal snowflakes will land soft as a feather,
The chandeliers formed by ice on bare branches
Are as smooth to the touch as sueded leather.

Sparkling like a field of glitter in the sun,
More beautiful and elegant than a party dress,
Sleek, fitting, hugging the roundness of the earth,
Letting the sun and moon, the full curves caress.

Equal to diamonds in the beauty of reflection,
The facets throwing off the light of a rainbow,
Using the colors of the sky as a background,
Shades of pink and blue enhance every tiny glow.

More stunning than anything man can design,
It will fill the mind with a sense of awe,
And feelings of humility when the scene is viewed,
For each snowflake is a thing of beauty, so raw.

We have this wonder for just a few months
And then the frost melts into the earth,
But these riches from us have not been stolen,
For spring raindrops of opal
shall soon show off their worth.

Let Me Be Yours

You can show me the mysteries of life.
All those stories that are old and new.
The ones that are close to your heart.
Ones special and dear to you.

Whisk me away to lands and dreams unknown.
Where someone like me can't go alone.
Show me things only you can see.
Places only you can go.

Then you can tell me how to make time stop.
We can kiss and hold each other tight.
Get rid of the fears that remain.
And sleep deeply through the night.

You can let yourself see I mean no harm.
Admit to yourself I'm not a fake.
Because if I were to hurt you.
Not only your heart would break.

Little Boy Scared

Your face told us the truth about you,
Your beautiful face and innocent soul,
When you became too big for it all,
You had to change your goal.

There was nothing wrong with your mind,
Nor anything you created with your hands,
You just outgrew your halo and wings
And began to believe no one understands.

The ones who loved you the best and
knew that day would come,
Understood your desire to correct everything
before you died,
Your life became an obstacle course
that no one could traverse,
But you, dear child, could have and would have
almost anything you tried.

There was more than one person
who wanted to help you,
But, in your generosity,
you didn't want to cause more pain.
If only we had known we could have told you to stop,
Still we watched you walk away from us
down that lonely lane.

We envy your escape from the nightmare of life,
But why couldn't you have stayed a little longer?
Now we must continue on our appointed paths,
We thank you,
for through you, we were able to be stronger.

Loneliness

Whimpers from a voice that cannot be heard,
Salty tears from eyes that cannot see,
Hands cold before a flame that gives no heat,
Living a life one would rather not be.

Sun shining on a face turned away,
Rest sought desperately every night,
Paper and pen lying nearby,
Meant for letters that no one will write.

Back hunched under a load so heavy,
Muscles weary from work never done,
Never sharing happiness for two,
And only enough sadness for one.

Laughter coming from unseen others,
Giving pity because not one cared,
Running from a love hidden 'til now,
Too ashamed for the soul to be bared.

Arms open to hug a pile of rags,
The only warmth given in reply,
A mind that cannot have happy dreams,
It's just a person waiting to die.

Look Within

At the opposite ends of the world we met,
Only to find we were neighbors in our hearts,
We are so much alike it shocked even us,
Two people running around trying to find lost parts.

These parts were the children
who deserved more than they got,
They were cheated whether through death or even worse,
Wearing their "imperfections" where everyone can see,
Leaving their families worrying and parents terse.

Youth being challenged before they know the word,
Unaware of the ugly and mean side of life,
Looking around with eyes innocent and pure,
Naïve and sweet not planning to live in strife.

Are you the one who will destroy their kindness?
Or, are you the one who will make them feel lesser?
Will you be able to live with yourself and others?
Please, feel badly and run to your confessor.

Then open your eyes and look at the little ones,
Be grateful you can see them before they're not here;
We have already missed out on too many others,
So many lives ended before the end of the year.

Written for a "Little One"

Me

When will any of you think of me first?
Haven't I been there for each and all of you?
If this isn't so then, tell me about it,
For I feel these words I've written are true.

When do I become a priority?
I know how important education is,
For I, too, want to learn as much as I can,
My learning more, is as important as his.

My studies will not change anyone's life,
Writing a book to some is "no big thing,"
With all I can't do, I liked the idea
Of bringing a song to the world that cannot sing.

I don't have much to leave my loved ones,
All I have is my love and a weird background,
Just a few trinkets and a love of the arts,
And pride in the fact they helped the world go 'round.

I hope I will leave the earth a better place,
But if money is what it takes, I've lost the race.

Melancholia

Identification with melancholia is extreme,
Songs depicting sadness bring memories filled with tears,
Memories from my youth yet surprisingly
not young in content,
Pains associated with adult emotions seem prevalent.

Total recall of ideas and moods are set to or
Caused by situation come rushing forth,
When the melody is familiar.

Strange, I always thought myself heartless
when adolescent,
Nothing could be more untrue.

Even more disturbing is the realization
that the same things sorrow me,
Stray puppies and cats
make me wish I could care for them all,
People all alone tear me apart,
Proper love I have for each.

Yet I also know that I want to give this love
With the hope that a small part shall be returned,
I give of myself selfishly,
But have never been so hurt as to not go on giving.

My B-Boy, All Mine

I have lost yet another of my loved ones,
Oh, please let his soul wait for me,
He has left a hole in my heart,
That can be filled by no one else than he.

My eyes fill with tears at the thought of you,
My breath becomes trapped in my chest,
Entering the kitchen is so lonely now,
I so miss my milk addicted pest.

My bony buddy, I wish I could hold you again,
I can't get you out of my mind,
I can picture your perfect cat nose so clearly,
A more special cat, I will never find.

You needed me almost as much as I needed you,
So your mother entrusted you to me,
From the beginning you were a gift,
For your life was a daily thank you, you see.

I hope you knew how very much I loved you,
But "loved" is wrong because you, I still love,
I wish I knew if you could understand,
And you are smiling at me from above.

My Love

Someone became a part of me that day long ago,
It felt so very right,
Or maybe he was always there, just in the back,
And just shy of the light.

He was there always, if I'm not mistaken,
Love was spontaneous,
I knew he was my past, my now and my future,
Yet, it was mysterious.

I love him in a way that will last forever,
Tomorrow has always,
He owns my heart, my soul and occupies my mind,
And the rest of my days.

He is my good days and good time until my death,
I thank the Lord above,
For letting me be in his heart and soul as well,
The word for this is love.

My New Bundle Of Joy, Belinda

How does one prepare for a third miracle in life?
And you, darling Belinda, truly are one.
And how does one show God how much
we wish to thank Him?
Oh, surely the words 'thank you' cannot be overdone.

There are many things about you
that make my heart swell.
From that crazy hairdo to your eyes so blue,
They are etched so deeply in my soul and mind,
That I know each memory of you is real and true.

You did not come alone when you came into this world,
With you, you brought wonder and joy
and thoughts of the past,
All things you do everyday are, as if, branded
In the book of time, your name already cast.

Time passes by so quickly that some things have faded,
One page, I see your parents, when like you,
they were small.
They were soft and smooth,
I thought they would always be so,
Yet, when I turn the page, they appear quite tall.

So, don't rush to grow up for time will do that for you,
And you will find you're a grandparent before you know,
Let my tears of joy blur the edges of now and then,
And please, clear my eyes so that I may see tomorrow.

My Personal Friend, My Lady

She didn't look that big when I was still at sea,
When I got closer, the Lady became larger than life.
I looked around but her husband was not to be seen,
Surely that lady had to be somebody's wife.

A few days later, she wasn't quite as scary,
So I went back to meet the lady on the island,
Well, that didn't seem to be something too hard to do,
For indeed, the lady seemed to be very kind and grand.

The guards opened the doors and let me go inside,
I looked up and realized she had many stairs to climb,
It was a dare but I felt up to the challenge,
The first flight seemed to go well and I had lots of time.

Flight two came to be a great deal longer and higher,
Looking up I saw only more and more staircases,
I tried to make it a game
and I was going to be the winner,
It actually became sort of like going through mazes.

The third flight of stairs were absolutely unbearable,
I didn't seem to be making any progress at all,
I grabbed the banister and hung on for dear life,
I didn't want to embarrass myself by taking a fall.

The stairs of flight four were a complete disaster,
Now the main and overwhelming feelings were fears,
Suddenly hands held me tightly and were comforting,
Slowly I felt safe and someone wiped away my tears.

I turned around and reached up
for the big hand of the Lady,
I knew that I would never be able
to hold or shake her hand,
But I was happy I had at least gotten to say hello
And that big Lady and I would live in the same land.

That event is factual as I'm sure you've figured out,
There are some facts
that most natural Americans don't know,
Most of us after the war, we had no homes anymore,
But now I live in America and will forever remain so.

My Schnooshakapanzers

My bow-legged ball of fur,
I miss you so very badly.
I think of you quite often.
And then smile very sadly.

The only comfort I have when it comes to you,
Is that I know you didn't suffer from any pains.
I know your joints ached and you moved stiffly,
Especially when it rained.

The vet said she could tell you were greatly loved,
You were given lots of love and care,
That you were a beautiful cat,
With lots of fun to share.

But, at times, I still can see you playing,
Out of the corner of my eye,
So I haven't really lost you,
I've never said good-by.

One day we'll be together again,
We will have many more times of fun,
And, I'll still let you sleep on my pillow,
And hold you very close, to be as one.

May 17, 1995

My Second New Bundle Of Joy, Tessa

So you thought I forgot to write a poem about you,
How could I not write about the smilingest baby?
Who but Tessa can smile so charmingly yet shy,
Who else can have such an innocent look but she?

In mere human time, you are miracle number four,
But don't let that fool you, you are all so different,
Happy smiles you all wear so beautifully,
As roses wear different shades, all a different scent.

Tessa, you captivate the hearts of everyone,
Like your parents and sister who came before you,
But, please don't think you are identical to any of them,
You are as special and as wonderful, this is true.

Since you've moved away,
I don't see you as often as I would like,
I must rely on pictures and memories to see you,
This isn't fair since you grow more lovely every day,
Not even time can change your smile or eyes of blue.

Can I tell you a secret to share with your sister?
I want to see much more of her and of you,
Of course I love your parents, I do most sincerely,
But neither are as precious as your sister and you!

Never Able To Do It Right

I'm in a quandary when it comes to living,
I seem to be very badly equipped for this world,
Just when I think I'm doing fine, I'm not doing okay;
I become like a flag that's not quite unfurled.

When I feel that perhaps I should be more elegant,
It seems that I always miss the important beat,
When I hold back my true feelings I have for others,
I get thrown around as if I were a can in the street.

I'm not feeling sorry for myself, it's quite the opposite,
It's for others that I must apologize to,
There doesn't seem to be anyone that can just let me be,
To everyone I have hurt or neglected,
I'm apologizing to you.

Never Back

The years of life keep parading by,
No one could stop them even if they try,
Slowing time is an impossibility,
Nothing can open that lock without the key.

Photographs give us a bit of the past,
Cheap reminders of times that didn't last,
Memories are given a nudge to find
All the details are hidden in the mind.

Who has not looked at a picture of when,
And asked "Did I really look like that then?"
Some of us see ourselves as young and gay,
Wishing that we could return to that day.

The rest of us don't think it was that nice,
And are relieved we won't go through it twice.
We are forced to see that youth is what we lack,
Time only goes forward, it never goes back.

Night Games

Wading into sunset,
facing the harsh glare of the sun,
Glad that day was over,
that all chores had been done.

Dark loomed on the horizon,
evening turned into night,
Clouds bowed out of the way,
letting stars become the light.

Searching for a perfect seat,
thus finding the highest hill,
Kneeling at the top,
arms resting on nature's windowsill.

Eyes wide as can be,
and trying to calm a heart wildly pounding,
Filled with excitement and awe,
engulfed by a scene, oh, so astounding.

The stars twinkled and
danced into their appointed shapes,
The sky cloaked in ebony,
to form the velvety drapes.

Then gazing over a shoulder,
hoping to glimpse the moon,
There it was in its roundness,
looking like a balloon.

Bobbing away to flee from the sun,
in their nightly game of hide and seek,
The moon slipped behind a veil of clouds,
looking out just for a peek.

The moon soon grew weary,
and was once more caught by the sun,
For, as it always was by the sun,
the game had been won.

Now wading into the sunrise,
facing the soft, muted sphere,
Smug in the knowledge the game wasn't over,
it was just a retreat.

No Justice

A great wrong happened that day
more than forty years past,
They attempted to cover it up
but hiding their feelings didn't last.
They played all the right games
and soon thought the mold was cast,
But nature finally took over and began to set things right,
leaving them aghast.

At first, lost and confused,
it didn't really know what to be,
Unfortunately, the stage was set
making it crucial to act right to stay free,
But the heart kept quiet and prayed that the role
was easier to be than she,
With her mind and her soul growing
she soon found the best thing to be.

Being Me is a very hard way to go,
I didn't perform as they were used to seeing,
I didn't actually rebel but I did do it my way,
leaving me asking if I was truly worth being.
I kept on saying, "Hey, I'm a good person,"
they kept saying no, leaving me livid and seething,
I will follow your rules only, said I, when north is south,
east is west and hell starts freezing.

So now I am truly me and feeling something special,
I'm happy, I'm content and very, very proud,
I will not back down when told to be quiet,
on the contrary, I will speak loud,
I will not walk around feeling ashamed
nor will I keep my head bowed,
For now I am me and I'm somebody!
Boy, oh, boy, am I proud.

Isanne Zoller

No Place For Me

Here?
Is certainly not where I belong,
Insults and cruelty are visitors everyday,
And it's getting harder to be strong.

> *There?*
> *Is no different than where I am today,*
> *Just a change of faces but still no love,*
> *People can't love me is all I can say.*

> > *Nowhere!*
> > *Is there perpetual kindness and care,*
> > *I guess these are things I'll never have,*
> > *From what I've experienced, they are rare.*

If you understand what I have written,
Then you'll agree with my conclusion,
There is no such thing as true happiness,
All good things are just an illusion.

Not Anymore!

Pushed to the back one too many times,
Stepped on because of someone else's mood,
Expected to always take what others give,
Being spoken to in a manner so rude.

Just living their lives as if only they count,
Cutting you off when it's your turn to speak,
Only they deserve to be treated with kid gloves,
And, if you don't agree, they freak.

Since they concern themselves with themselves,
They ignore anything and everything someone might do,
They don't hesitate to be cruel because of their mess,
But never do they listen when you need to talk about you.

No matter how one may try to help,
They prefer to be the eternal victim forever,
They hide behind a tragedy, though real,
But you cannot talk about your own pain, ever.

Some people have a hard time with their lives,
Through no fault of their own,
But they censor your words before they are said,
And then wonder why they're all alone.

Once

She looked askance at him while he slept,
And wondered what had happened to all the years.
She tried not to remember the secrets that she kept,
None-the-less, memories caused the flooding of tears.

There were good times that they shared,
But, hey, couldn't assuage the bad,
She was angry because she knew she cared,
Still, the anger made her feel sad.

There was a time in her life when laughter came free,
She just couldn't recall how it felt.
Did people really say, could it actually be,
That the melody, your heart, it would melt?

To protect her heart, she holds herself tight,
And gently rocks herself to help ease the pain.
Each day she awakens and prepares for the fight,
Knowing that today is the day she may be slain.

Once she was happy, elated and gay,
But now she is lonely, so tired and weak,
Once she was beautiful, or so they would say,
Now she is ugly and looks as a freak.

She was born old and wanted to find something
That would make her carefree and feel young,
She wanted to leap and fly as the whole world would ring,
With the sound of her music as her song was sung.

One Of Life's Absurdities

The family gathered around the chocolate,
Most didn't really want a bite,
Some wanted it because Mom was eating,
Some did want a little taste just to be polite.

This scenario occurs several times a day,
It has reached the point of total boredom,
The group has become caught in a rut,
It angers a few but is still enjoyed by some.

How long this will continue, who can tell,
It has become a ritual of sorts,
Most often the throng wants the foreplay
Long before it's time for the tortes.

The gathering starts losing its size,
A few turn their heads in case there is more,
Two are totally unconcerned with the play,
One is still quite upset and struts out the door.

Each time this happens, they go through the moves,
They won't deal with the reality of the facts,
She tries to explain that in this situation
Some of us are humans and some of us are cats.

Opened Eyes

*There were so many days
when I trusted it would go well.
But there you arrived, after two in the night.
My hunger had disappeared and
you had broken my heart.
It never seemed to you that what you did,
wasn't all right.*

*I wasn't prepared for any of these problems.
My ignorance was laughed at and I was stupid.
In some things I was very naïve.
But then, you were no cupid.*

*I accepted my mistakes and tried to do better.
I did almost anything to make you want me.
By then, I finally was adult enough to raise a child.
But I still wanted the man I loved, to love me.*

*So many said it was a waste of my time.
Sometimes, I felt they were indeed right.
And you came home just to be our family.
Play and laugh and hold me all night.*

*You left me again for something I couldn't compete with.
You swore I was number one for you.
Instead of waiting for you to return my life.
I had to make one without you.*

Others

*The Condemned – Those who have given more than was
    ever given to them
The Blessed – Those who were chosen to never suffer
    heartache
The Cursed – Those who have been aware of each act but
    say nothing
The Joyful – Those who have closed their minds to accept
    all that was taken
By others.*

*The Tragic – Those who have believed only what they
    wanted to believe
The Trusting – Those who have not yet accepted the facts
    of reality
The Used – Those who have, despite themselves, allowed
    others to be cruel
The Deceitful – Those who have lied to the very ones that
    cared
For others.*

*The Tortured – Those who have been just shy of evil but,
    not always
The Clowns – Those who have learned to laugh no
    matter what has happened
The Escapees – Those who have buried their heads in the
    sands of time
The Lonely – Those who have done their best to please
    and cater to
Others.*

Our Loss

We have all shared a loss of someone special,
She was known better by some, but, loved by us all,
She was gentle and taught this to her children,
And we will all miss being able to give her a call.

I personally didn't know her as well as I wished,
But I have sweet memories that go back thirty-one years,
Oh, how she could make me giggle and laugh,
And now, she's gone, but she left me with only tears.

There are stories we all could tell,
And many things we'd all like to have shared.
But right now, we are better off just holding these
thoughts dear,
I hope she knows how very much we cared.

I feel the best way to show this is to be like her,
She was strong when her beloved passed away,
And she was gentle when others needed comfort,
So let's think about this woman
and her kindness every day.

This family knows how to care for our loved ones,
And no one is too lazy to help each other,
This loved woman gave all of us no matter what,
So, let's make sure we are there for one another.

Our Unwelcome Pain

Why did you stop caring about our feelings
That, with your encouragement grew?
After placing our hearts on our sleeves,
You let us know that with us, you were through.

Our words pleased you enough that you wanted more,
With our rhymes, we kept you fed;
All of us tried our hardest so you would like us,
In return, all we got was a pat on the head.

We trusted you and gave you our respect,
All of us competing to be your number one,
These many years lo, we went along with it,
Hoping, for you, reading what we wrote, was fun.

We came together at your ever changing address,
We listened to every word you spoke,
Oh, how we thought you wanted us with you,
That week-end, do you know how many hearts you broke?

You probably don't realize how betrayed we felt,
Not one minute did you have to listen to our dreams,
You also made sure that you never had to face us,
You made sure that you were too far away
to hear our screams.

By making sure we could never touch you,
You may just have started preparing your own end,
For even if you are the largest society,
There are others to whom, our peers, we can send.

Every person who dealt with you was treated unfairly,
Our normal lives were what we wanted to escape from,
Bus drivers, housewives, sales clerks and mechanics,
You treated all of us as if we were dumb.

There is not enough kindness in this ugly world,
There is too much suffering we must endure,
But, you knew exactly how to find our weakness,
You knew how to make us feel secure.

We will not stop writing our lovely words,
But, dear people, prepare yourselves for a change,
For now it is our turn to treat you poorly,
For now it is our turn to make you feel unwelcome
and strange.

The promises you made were never meant to keep,
Still, I thought it was beneath you to be cruel,
You and your assistants did what you set out to do,
You played us for a collective fool.

Peace

A time and place where no overt war is happening,
A way of life that leaves our consciousness at rest,
A sense of security in the fact the enemy has left,
Leaving the world behaving at its very best.

Don't be fooled by the meetings of our chosen leaders,
They only try to pacify our anxiety,
For everyone not invited to these lofty sessions,
They could be chatting, for all we know,
having a cup of tea.

Tell me that someone cares about the earth's future,
Where could everyone go if something ugly would occur?
Do all the past problems of man mean the end of life?
Do we have to stop life by having mankind neutered?

Must we continue propagating the evil side?
Why can't we just stop hating and killing each other?
Who is finally going to take the words to heart
About who is truly and will always be our brother?

Having suffered the trickling down effect of World War II,
I pray that the atrocities will never be repeated,
According to the plans, there will never be an "again,"
It's finally safe for the ground to be reseeded.

Quiet Passions

*Mellow feel I
Being gently caressed by the music
Within and about me.
Warm with love
Feelings of security abound.
I am lulled into peace,
Bliss,
By soothing emotions.*

*Softly, I show my love to him
Who is willing to see,
Feel my comfort, taste my joy.
Inhale my perfume of passion.
Accept my love
As I receive yours,
Greedily and desperately.*

Sales!

Back to school shouted all the store sales,
Ten percent off all clothing for males.
Buy one, fifty percent all the rest,
But nothing off the very best!

So when it comes to women's clothing,
Most styles cause a great deal of loathing.
While some things on their hangers look nice,
Still, you should try them on twice!

Some clothes hang as rags if you're too thin,
If you're obese, you just never win.
When you're in between things fit so right,
But, as for me, I'll just say Good Night!!

Save Your Loved Ones!

Animal advocates say get your pet neutered or spayed,
It won't be long before they've said that
too many eggs have been laid.
Are we a society where pets
will soon be a thing of the past?

I, for one, think it's safe to assume
that these people do mean well,
And, if that indeed there are many animals
that LIVE IN HELL,
But, if we do what they say,
how long would these species last?

How many of our children
have never petted a dog or a cat?
Have never seen a cardinal fly or
heard a woodpecker's rap?
Don't you know that the populations of these
are dwindling fast?

Do your children know that blue jays are birds
and not just a baseball team?
Or do they know that there are not as many geese
as it may seem?
That the small number of these
would leave you in horror and aghast?

Please do think it over carefully
before you do as they say,
Put it off 'til tomorrow and then watch the animals play,
Because you must remember the species
are really dwindling fast!!

Senses

Cast your fate upon the shore,
Watch waves take it out to sea,
Take your dreams and toss them toward the sky,
The stars will catch them, most definitely.

Look around and see the world,
Listen to the birds sing to you,
Relish a nap on a bed of leaves,
Touch the blades of grass that grow anew.

Be sure to see the flowers,
And smell the scents so delightful,
Sit beneath a weeping willow tree,
All of nature, o, so wonderful.

Don't forget to share this joy,
With someone beside you it's nice,
For to see everything through their eyes,
Then the pleasure for you has grown by twice.

Pretend you're a child again,
Remember how it was then,
Collecting lightening bugs in a jar,
Recall the happiness of way back when.

Sisters

The relationship of sisters is in every way unique,
No one else can share your life the way they do.
The few years in ages melt to nothing as you grow older,
And no one else can have the same memories as you.

It is because of this that they will always be there,
But it is also because of this, losing them is so sad,
Just picture the way they moved their hands while talking
And the funny faces and noises that drove you mad.

These memories can bring a twinkle to your eye,
a smile to your face,
But, unfortunately,
these memories can also make you cry,
But, if each smile grows wider and
each laugh lasts longer,
The life and love you two shared will truly never die.

Thank You

Brown leaves lying on white snow like war victims,
Some trees are sadly, totally bare,
Maples and oaks no longer in competition,
While all the saplings are just standing there.

Still more casualties float by the window,
Looking more pained than the one before,
Each cruelly stabbed by an icicle of winter,
Never bleeding though cut to the core.

But then a softer snow falls covering all,
Providing a bed for everything,
Even the wind quiets down until all is silent,
All anticipating what the new season will bring.

Squirrels run helter skelter looking for nuts,
Birds of all sizes follow close by,
Readying the world for the miracle of life,
Preparing for that life before they die.

There's nothing here on earth quite so beautiful,
No smell as good or jewel so rare,
As the love of family so rich and abundant,
Goodness and kindness for all to share.

Thank you God, for all.

That Tablecloth

Parents are not people who watch you grow,
They are there to give you love
and teach you many things,
Some of these things you see and some you get to know,
But the best of what you learn from them
is what love brings.

Your folks invite you to join them when times are merry,
Teach you the difference between right and wrong,
To smile when you're glad and
hold you when things are scary.
They tell you when it's time for silence
and time for song.

Your mom and dad gave you all
many times that were fun,
Things that made you laugh so hard
it almost made you cry,
But there was something that you did
that was second to none,
And those memories will stay with you until you die.

When the eldest of you children
was only three months old,
That camping tablecloth became part of the family,
Remember all the meals served in the heat and the cold,
How much love there was
and how much there will always be.

As you get older, memories can begin to fade,
But if you keep doing those things
they will always be there,
Make sure you don't forget
all those happy times you made,
Don't be selfish with the love you have
and always can share.

This poem was written by request for a friend.

Isanne Zoller

The Beauty Of Winter

Leaves dancing tarantellas along the curb,
More performing pirouettes to the ground,
Giving their final performance of the year,
The bare trees applauding, the last autumn sound.

Then all you hear is the silence of the pause,
Even as the air seems not to move at all,
Tiny sprites of snow start to jump all around,
Playing tricks on your eyes, you don't see them fall.

And just when you decide you'll look away,
The corps of ballet begins floating into view,
Each larger than the one before it,
Spiraling toward the windows just to tease you.

Starting to giggle as when you were a child,
You catch your breath as flakes curtsey before you,
Eyes never leaving the scene, you slowly nod,
Letting them know you give each snowflake its due.

Riveted to the spot, they leave you speechless,
Spinning and leaping, they dance their last dance,
Gracefully they imprint their miracle in your mind,
Knowing they let you see them was not by chance.

The Botanical Secret

Capable of scientific analyzation,
Your complexities hidden within explanations,
Soft, you command attention
By mere existence.

Multi-formed, multi-hued,
So basic and similar,
The ever-present comfort of life,
It's past, it's now and future.

Absorbed by your extensions,
Subtly controlling man by obscure threats,
Insure my survival lest you kill yourself,
Echoes from each appendage.

Care is given because guilt is too burdensome.

Isanne Zoller

The Child

The child everyone wants is not always who we get,
We still love them dearly but the love isn't given back,
As parents, most of us try our hardest to be good,
But there must be something that we lack.

Our children look at us as if we are stupid,
Especially when they have one or more of their own,
They must believe they were born knowing everything
And we were as useful to them as a drone.

True not all of us were experts before their births,
But most of us did truly try our best,
And just when it became fun for us,
They up and left the nest.

Suddenly, nothing we parents did was ever correct,
They had learned automatically
how to do everything right,
Now the only thing our children would like
Is for us to just drop out of sight.

I wish the children would realize
that their lives were gifts,
Maybe they didn't get all the things everyone else had,
But from their parents, they were given all we could give,
The fact that they don't understand,
This is what makes me sad.

The Cycle Of Nature

The stubble of trees on the chin of the bluff,
The sheen of ice on its brow,
Rivulets like tears from its eyes,
All these doth winter man mountain endow.

Nature's dales are bare and shrubs are gnarled,
Its farmlands no longer beautiful,
The word "ugly" becomes the adjective used,
And beauty's return quite doubtful.

All surfaces gleaming in the rays of the sun
Are only a mockery of a sky so blue,
For the ground stays frozen and
the cold wind still blows,
When warm weather will return, there isn't a clue.

Then suddenly, the stubble becomes a beard,
And the glens are sported with reds and greens,
The sun now shines giving warmth to the earth,
Everything thought before to only be in dreams.

We thank you God, for all we hold dear,
All living things have made it through another year.

The Day

The children have all grown,
And now they have lives of their own.
The rest of us have grown gentle,
For we know that life is but a rental.
Though tribulations on earth we must meet,
The wealth we are given in heaven is sweet.
Think of the joy and happiness in the hereafter,
Being with all of our loved ones, hearing their laughter.

Yes, there are many roads and paths but only one,
the true way,
For if in His steps we walk,
we shan't be lost on Judgment Day.

For when that day comes we must all prepare,
Remember our acts and those in need of repair,
With our burdens lightened and
our minds thinking clearer,
The Lord, heaven and loved ones
will be that much nearer.

The End Of A Love

Did you ever experience a sad farewell?
Sometimes people say it turns out to be for the best,
The problem is if only one wants to part,
Then behaving civilly is no more than a test.

To the one leaving, the past was a waste of time,
To the one left behind, the past becomes everything,
For them, what once felt right becomes a fantasy,
All things that were wrong become reduced to nothing.

Many people feel that death is preferable,
No reason can justify living when the other one goes,
It leaves some feel that their lives are useless,
Everyone around them turn from friends to foes.

How can one person turn into a cold-hearted monster?
When exactly is the moment that true love dies?
Is there a look or a sigh that relays that message?
Or do we just know the one who is left behind
is the one that cries.

Isanne Zoller

The Four Seasons

Spring:
Raindrops of opal dripping gently to the earth.

Summer:
Leaves of jade cooling in the hot sun.

Autumn:
Topaz leaves dancing tarantellas along the ground.

Winter:
Chandeliers of ice cascading from all branches.

The Girls Of Summer

The girls of summer have never changed,
They are as frisky and happy as always,
Though some days aren't as much fun
But, there is always a smile for all days.

Life has not always been kind to them,
But it's never knocked them down,
When they looked as though they were,
They could still teach the other women in town.

The girls will be girls forever for their hearts
are filled with love,
Not a single young woman can do
what these girls have done,
They raised their families,
taught them how to be good people,
And every battle they undertook, they definitely won.

There aren't any more girls of summer,
We are neither as strong nor as wise as they still are,
If we're quiet, listen carefully, and look at the sky,
We will always have them as our lucky stars.

The Last Victim

I am a victim of the war and its finality
Though I wasn't even a thought or being then,
My mind never lies to or plays tricks on me,
I knew it was going to be, I just didn't know when.

When I tell you my story, you'll say, "Of course,"
Then I'll say, "It's true" and you'll say, "Yeah, right,"
But let's stop there for we're wasting time,
We could be disputing this all through the night.

Instead, think how every family has a historian,
And I am the one for my ancestry.
It wasn't something I elected to do,
But now it is a story that does include me.

There is an avalanche of emotions that was passed down,
The pain started before the war, though all were still alive,
There was one that was injured critically,
And she, she was the center of the hive.

So from spouse and children to cousins twice removed,
All their lives suffered without her existence,
So that's why I can say truthfully,
I lived through the war giving no resistance.

The Library

The little children have the right attitude
That being surrounded by books should be fun
That takes the young who grow to be
Adults to claim the world is at their fingertips.

Their enthusiasm brings to life their
Love as the curiosity nurtures
Blossoms of intelligence bordering
All who choose to partake of the wine of the printed word.

A rush was never so strong as the
Smell of ink and binders' glue creating
A headiness no drug could compare to
Its permanent place in a building of knowledge.

Nothing can compete with the places of
Travel that flies to spots on the earth and down
To the core of elements no one knew
Before entering the magic land so old.

The Man Made Of Music

The little one sat unable to reach the pedals,
Then the muse of music gave him a lift,
And without having to try to play, he just did,
Because God gave him a special gift.

There was a love for the arts in his entire family,
And he started absorbing and uniting with every note,
But even the adults couldn't keep up with him,
For even at his young age, it was music he also wrote.

This child breathed the old masters taking on their style,
And as he became more proficient, he also found his way,
He took so much pleasure in it,
he had to share it with others,
And from then on, he taught others
to have music every day.

Each student, no matter how old or young,
caught his fervor,
Most, as my sister and I could tell,
became good but he was always better.
We would always ask our father
could he play it once more,
So that we too could learn to play it to the letter.

If that term seems strange to you, then I will explain,
As you are hearing these words, picture them as love,
And then perhaps you can begin to understand,
All these notes he has played were his mail from above.

July 11, 2001

The Oneness

Pressed against the window feeling the warmth,
Wondering how they could survive without the breeze,
Gasping, then gulping, the air barely moves,
But they will stay that way until it's time to freeze.

Sweltering in the season that starts their demise,
There isn't a way to stop this cycle really,
Life is a continuing repetition ever,
And all of nature has chosen it quite freely.

Though turning into colors of fire,
It certainly looks as if it caused no pain,
Still as a human being I can only guess,
If all can be cooled by a deluge of rain.

O, wouldn't it be wonderful if man could change too,
Then think of how lovely the entire world would be,
For if there would be a race that included all,
Every living thing would be beautiful to see.

The Pain

There is a pain that hurts more than most,
It's an ache that seems to never go away,
You try to sleep and pray the hurt will ease,
But, you awake to face reality of one more day.

There are no signs on the body to explain it,
There is nothing for a doctor to see on the outside,
Even when a surgeon would find nothing,
For there's nothing wrong on the inside.

It's a pain so excruciating some will prefer insanity,
Some will pray to God to take their lives as well,
Others will say it happens to everyone,
More will feel they've been sent to hell.

Some men will be sad but can go on living,
Some women will also be able to deal with it,
In my mind it makes these people selfish and mean,
With brains no larger than a cherry pit.

There are many things that can kill the body,
Things such as a knife or a well-aimed bullet hole,
But there are also weapons, such as cruel words,
That will cause the death of a human's soul.

The Past Of Tomorrow's Love

I quietly watched as the little girl and boy,
Finally put away their very last toy.

Now with arms empty and hearts slightly broken,
They turned to each other and these words were spoken,

"I'll care for you always, for the rest of my life,
If you will just promise to become my wife."

She turned to him softly saying, "I feel just the same,
I would be happy and honored to share with you
your name."

With eyes full of innocence and oh, so very blue,
They whispered the words, "I love you true."

I quietly watched as they made promises and vows
To love each other always just as they did now.

Shortly thereafter, the toys came out again,
Some to be played with, if that day it should rain.

Now it was their turn to wait for the day,
When, once again, the toys would all be put away.

With eyes not so innocent, yet, still oh, so blue,
They whispered the words, "I still love you true."

The Past Of Tomorrow's Love
Part 2

I quietly watched as the little girl and boy,
Finally put away their very last toy.

Now with arms empty and hearts slightly broken,
They turned to each other and these words were spoken,

"I'll care for you always for the rest of my life,
If you will just promise to become my wife."

She turned to him softly saying, "I feel just the same,
I would be happy and honored to share with you
your name."

With eyes full of innocence and oh, so very blue,
They whispered the words, "I love you true."

I quietly watched as they made promises and vowed,
To love each other always, just as they did now.

Shortly thereafter, the toys came out again,
Some to be played with if that day it should rain.

Now it was their turn to wait for the day,
When, once again, the toys would all be put away.

With eyes not so innocent but, still, oh, so very blue,
They whispered the words, "I still love you true."

For them, the time will come more quickly
than they think,
For children are always just at the brink.

No matter how carefully it is planned in their mind,
The lost teeth and too small clothes
will be all that's left behind.

Too soon college and real life will take them some day,
Followed again by vows and toys and going away,

Then others will watch quietly
as they hear new vows taken,
And they shall also feel a little forsaken.

But this is nothing more than the recycling of lives,
With sons becoming husbands and
daughters becoming wives.

Hopefully, years after they say the words, I do,
They, too, will still love each other true.

Again eyes full of innocence and oh, so very blue,
Will whisper the same words, I love you true.

The Simple Way

Let people see who you really are,
Don't be afraid to let them come near,
The very thing that worries your mind,
May also be what causes them, their fear.

A shift in the relationship must start now,
And must begin by holding out your hand,
Never let a moment pass by again,
Just jump in and don't care where you may land.

The Ugliest Obsession

The ugliest obsession is the one that makes you hurt me,
Meaning something you claim to be in jest
but you can't hide,
The amount of insults you deal
is only funny in your mind,
And, it is an example of your true feelings
that you denied.

Does it make you feel better
when you put me down to all?
Is that the only way you can feel more
the man in control?
Have you decided that this will always be your attitude?
Have you already planned when to give away
your very soul?

If you haven't given it yet, can you stop your cruelty?
Realize that whatever you do, the blame is yours,
true or not,
Can you live with your duplicity for the rest
of your time and more?
Try to remember there is no contest or
is that something you forgot?

In prayer the words come out awkwardly but are
heartfelt and true,
And believe it or not, these words are repeated everyday,
Please stop driving wedges into places that will only
destroy what we have,
Think before you try to make me sorry
that I ever thought to stay.

Isanne Zoller

The Ultimate Why

Why is everyone so busy running everyone's life?
Why aren't they taking care of their own?
Why can't they respect other's feelings?
Why is contention referred to as a bone?
Why is it said "If I were in your shoes...?"
Why can't they leave well enough alone?
Why do people say that practice makes perfect?
Why is it our skills we must hone?
Why is being tall considered great?
Why is it thought of as childish to eat an ice cream cone?
Why aren't we the ones worried about?
Why must we always pick up the phone?
Why when we get the gist must others still have to explain?
Why do people always feel all alone?
And why am I still writing this poem?

The Weed

*Walking alone in a nightmare of **pain**,*
*No matter **how** many pages I read,*
The words are washed away by all the rain.

*I feel as though I am in a **shaft** of black,*
*That deepens further with **each** minute of need,*
*But all the **tools** needed to climb out, I lack.*

*To **live**, one must have a great deal of energy,*
*To have this, one must **free** their garden of the weed,*
*The **weed** of pain that forces the garden to flee.*

*To flee **before** the flowers suffocate and die,*
*Before the **ground** can no longer accept a good seed,*
*And **definitely** before the good seeds even try.*

*I feel this **body** of mine is no more than a rental,*
*Unfortunately, my soul **must** follow where it may lead,*
*Leaving it will **certainly** not make me sentimental.*

*I have **craved** and longed for a moment*
of pain-free time,
*Oh, just **once** before I give up the fight and secede,*
*And give in to the **despair** and lose the desire to rhyme.*

The Wine Of Love

Let us complete one another,
Ne'er again to be whole by ourselves,
Be a part of me, share my life,
I offer you my only possession,
Myself.

And while I drink greedily of your wine,
I shall savor every drop and drain you not.
Don't be afraid to give yourself and thereby be empty,
For I shall replenish you with love,
My love.

The Woman Of The World

Oh! Nature! You are such a seductress!
First you tempt me with buds of light green,
Then you open your leaves and show me all the hues,
Placed way up high so they can't be reached,
You're keen!

My, Nature, you impossible vixen!
Taunting me with all the hues of greens,
You have an unending choice of Opalettes,
And dress all the trees as though they...
Were queens!

So, Nature, you really are a sadist!
You seduce with all those colors serene,
Then, just like a temperamental artist,
Bursting into a frenzy, wipe the...
Slate clean!

Oh! Nature! You really are divine!
Taking time as for a party you preen,
You put on colors that stun me completely!
Force all to pale by comparison,
You're mean!

Thoughts On God And Love

Serenity is a goal seldom aimed for,
More the pity, it is seldom thought of,
Words more attractive are on the top of everyone's list,
Such words as kind and gentle and above all, love.

People forget that inner peace can bring all three,
And they're so busy being busy,
that there is no time to think,
From the mouths of people of all ages
you're going to hear,
"I have to think of me and mine, the rest can go ...sink."

Why can't people remember that everyone
is "me and mine!"
Why don't they realize that being human
is also to be humane?
For and near, everyone is our family,
Different in so many ways but ultimately, the same...

When next you take a moment to look,
Open your eyes but also your heart and mind,
Realize that life is not easy but still harder for some,
Remember this and make your deeds
and your words kind.

All God's creatures have the right to live and be loved,
So, don't be angry with the bird that woke you too soon,
Take pleasure in the fact you woke to see the sun,
Bless the quiet night that shows you the moon.

Many scholars have said many wise things,
But, to me, a sensitive person said one thing
that's above the rest,
She put all conflicts and debates to rest,
All she said is "God is love."

Tips For Creating Pain

Loathing is such a delightfully vicious word
to say out loud,
If you know the definition for this word,
you should be proud,
When you don't know the true meaning
but know how to behave as if you do,
Then you are truly a sadistically evil person, yes, You!

You can glare across the table and
show that someone you abhor them,
Do make sure you let them know
they aren't even fit to touch your hem,
Don't forget to show increasing irritability
when you must repeat an answer,
And, whatever else you do, don't forget to act
as if you wish you were anyplace but there.

You must have a lame excuse for your behavior
no matter what they say,
Be prepared to deny anything,
whether you said it or did it, Okay?
Show no mercy when you go in for
the wickedest cruelty anyone would fear,
And, above all, don't forget you must act
as if you never saw the tear.

Vision

Eyes from hell looking up to the heavens,
Searching for something familiar or new,
Not knowing how to differentiate,
The good from the bad, the red from the blue.

A soul living ever in a darkness,
Can't be taught to see colors or the light,
When the only illumination in hell
Is a fire burning away all things from sight.

Tints and hues are merely shades of blackness,
Even flames seem only to flicker,
On high colors are complimentary,
While down there all appear to just bicker.

Above, reds and yellows are warm and kind,
G-D's palettes are gifts given to us all,
Below, evil has destroyed everything,
There is no spring, no summer, no fall.

But don't start worrying where it will all end,
Look around and just begin spreading love,
Below, there is nothing but ugliness,
Keep in mind, all good things come from above.

Was, Is, Will Be

Perhaps one day you will look and
then perhaps you'll see,
What is really going on and happening to me,
I'm not who I was nor who I will be,
But after it is done, I will finally be free.

You won't even listen though I tried to tell you so,
I've tried to warn you, tell exactly what I know,
It's hard to speak especially when I'm low,
Perhaps if you would listen, then you would definitely go.

My body is in misery, from every part I ache,
I have no reservoir of strength,
yet always from there you take,
You have your supply, for it is still a lake,
I beg of you draw from there, if only for my sake.

I know I shout too loudly and all too often cry,
But, when you turn to look at me,
I'm wiping my eyes dry,
I've told you many times and yes, I will still try,
My darling, you must know, my love, you just can't buy.

Just when you least expect it is when I'll go away,
First will be my soul. My body?, it can stay.
Then hopefully, mind, of this I truly pray,
I feel that this, for all, will be a happy day.

Where Have You Gone?

Where have you been hiding and from whom?
If you say us, then you have wasted a great deal of time,
You could've gotten your answers from
the ones that have loved you,
The most it would have cost you would've been a dime.

When you were already becoming a man
you asked us questions,
Not one do we recall not answering
even when they were tough,
But respond we did in the best way we knew how,
Even when the answers were not just not easy,
but, very rough.

It seems some of what you heard
you evidently didn't understand,
It seems, though, that most things you preferred
to not hear,
The answers were often something
you didn't want to know,
So you made up your versions and
listened in make-believe fear.

So now we are at a place
that resembles the Grand Canyon,
None of us knows what to say or not say,
You keep saying you have no problem with me,
And me? I'm always saying I love you everyday.

Why God Chose Me

When God chose me to be your mother,
He certainly chose the right one to be it, me.
He made the decision before you were even born.
When He decided, it meant He wanted it to be me.

He gave me the opportunity to have seven children,
And I fought to keep them all alive,
I did my best to help them and love them;
In the end, only you survived.

Let me tell you just how bad the pregnancy was,
While everyone else was watching fireworks,
I could only hear the bands,
I was given a due month and had to stay in bed.
Only then did He tell me, because,
I was putting your life in His hands.

If this sounds stupid, I can verify every word,
So, to my despair, I did stay in bed.
The only times I was allowed to go out
Was when I thought I was losing my head.

But, guess where I spent my entire pregnancy?
In bed for all ten months; I did this so I could have you.
I thought with your knowledge you could figure this out,
But I guess this means nothing to you.

I bled each day and constantly prayed to G-D,
Nothing meant more to me than you, who should survive,
Nothing meant more to me than you, my child,
Your living meant more to me than my life.

To make up for all the lost babies,
He gave one of His best ones to me.

Why Must This Happen?

I thought that holidays would be easier to deal with,
But, unfortunately, they are definitely not,
There does seem to be a curse upon me,
The tears that run down my cheeks burn hot.

I have tried to be casual about special days,
I look forward to them with nearly overwhelming joy,
They start out being happy times,
Like a child hoping for a toy.

We all start out with smiles on our faces,
Then someone becomes snide.
It hurts but I try very hard,
All those tears I try to hide.

When I was a child, holidays were sad,
And I have tried very hard to not repeat the pain,
But it has become something like wishing for snow,
Yet, all I've gotten is rain.

I would not prefer to have nothing to celebrate,
After all, we could celebrate on any old day,
But the calendars make it hard to pretend,
There's no Christmas or Mother's Day.

Your Beloved Future

A baby conceived in love, shall live in love,
Parents bonded in love, shall give this love.

Precious child, you will always know this,
There are so many people waiting for you,
So that we may show you our love,
Your family will forever give you, your due.

Your parents know there is magic
To the mathematics of this thing,
But try as they may, their two lives giving all,
Still add up to trice fold the love they bring.

With a history of love, kindness and more,
Little one, your start in life will be
Steeped in a specialness that is blessed,
You are a new branch on a strong family tree.

Tiny one, you will never be alone or lonely,
Your parents and family will always be there to go to,
A pillow made of happiness will comfort you,
If there are hard times you must go through.

Adored one, the cloak of love shall be yours always,
Wrap it tightly around you for all your days.

Zollers – Names

S - is for how Special you've grown to be.
T - is for how Tender you treat your family.
A - is for the Abundance of goodness you have inside.
C - is for the Constant love you have never denied.
E - is for the Elegance that within you, you hold.
Y - is for You, you're more valuable than gold.

B - is for your Beauty that you have within and without.
E - is for the Expressive heart that you must never doubt.
L - is for the way you Look deep into our souls.
I - is for the Intelligence you use to plan your goals.
N - is for the Nothing that you cannot do.
D - is for your Dreams, may they all come true.
A - is for Always, that's how you will be loved.

T - is for the Thoughts of love that are always forming in
your mind.
E - is for the Eager way your eyes show how you are kind.
R - is for the Richness of spirit and love that you give.
E - is for the Emotions you will have while you live.
S - is for the Sensitivity you show to all you see.
A - is for the Angel that you will forever be.

J - is for the Joy you bring to your children and wife.
O - is for the Open minded way you should go through life.
S - is for the Shine in your eyes when you look at your family.
E - is for the Expertise you strive for and will be.
P - is for the Peace of mind you receive from above.
H - is for the Hope you give to the important people you love.